21 Devotions from the Soul

All versions of the Bible scriptures used are noted next to the scriptures.

Editor and Book Cover Design: Penned Just Write LLC

Dedication

This book is dedicated to the faithful attendees of the MORNING J.O.Y. show. It is difficult to commit to getting up before the sun rises to prepare for a day filled with J.O.Y. BUT (Better Understand This), for those that do the reward is GREAT!

It is also dedicated to the future J.O.Y. Ambassadors who will make a commitment to not only start their day with J.O.Y. but spread the J.O.Y. to everyone that they come in contact with.

You all are AHHHHHmazing!

I pray God continues to bless you mightily.

JOYfully Yours,
Nicole Crews Carter

The JOurneY

"The JOY of God is your strength!" ***Nehemiah 8:10 NKJV***

In her quiet time with the Lord, Nicole Carter, "Ultimate J.O.Y. Leader", received a command to start a daily Clubhouse and Facebook show that encouraged the attendees to write out their J.O.Y. plan prior to starting their day. Although she was uncertain how it would turnout, she invited several people to assist her with moderating the room on Clubhouse.

That first day in March 2021, the room was a hit. Most of the people she invited attended the room and several people shared their J.O.Y. plan. However, the next day started very different. She started the room on Clubhouse and connected to Facebook at 5:58am. With the song "Joy" by Vashawn Mitchell playing in the background, she waited for others to join. The song ended at 6:01 with no one in the room. She played the song again, 6:05 still no one in the room. Around 6:08 she thought maybe she didn't hear the Lord clearly, so she ended the show on both Clubhouse and Facebook.

Just as she proceeded to leave her office a message came from Sister Deborah Phillips inquiring about the show. Nicole started the both Clubhouse and Facebook again. The Morning J.O.Y. show has been live every Monday – Friday for the last two years (except for a few days of vacation).

The first year, Nicole led the show encouraging attendees to share their J.O.Y. plan with fellow moderators providing encouragement, prayers and words of wisdom as the Holy Spirit urged. During the first year several people overcame anxiety, depression, lack of direction, insecurity, financial issues, career snags, relationship issues, lulls in their entrepreneurial endeavors, and the list goes on.

We celebrated the first anniversary with a virtual conference March 2022.

The show took on its first facelift April 2022. The weekly lineup changed to have various moderators' lead.

Motivational Monday – Nicole "J.O.Y. Leader"
Tools & Tips Tuesday – Michele Baran & Dr. Cindy Betts
Worship Wednesday – Darren Lyons & Latasha Toney
Thankful Thursday – Elisa Daguanno & Joy Kitango-Diabo
Faithful Friday – Janice Burton & Eileen Tarpley Williams

We celebrated the second anniversary with an in-person conference with presentations by Pastor Craig, Pastor Chris, Andrea Merriman, Neva Brooks, Psalmist Sidney Price, Quint Price, and our praise team, Janice, Elisa, & Eileen.

The next major change occurred April 2023. Along with a few familiar faces, we added a couple of new voices.

Motivational Monday Book Review – Nicole & Leigh Harold
Guest Speaker Tuesday – Janice Burton & Eileen Williams
Watcha Wanna Know Wednesday – Michele B. & Dr. Cindy
Scripture & Listening Lounge – Darren Lyons & Elisa Daguanno
Game Day FriYAY – Coach Jacqui & The Joyful One

We also have several supporting moderators, Neva Brooks, Yolanda Coleman Brown, Mari Sakamoto, Rick Kalamon, Pastor Craig Carter, Pastor Chris Campbell, and Elder Sylvester Durham. We've added a prayer wall and continue making strategic Spiritual partnerships.

As we continue our J.O.Y. JOurneY, we expect God to move in miraculous ways in the lives of His people.

How the J.O.Y. Plan Works

After reading the devotional for the day, follow the recommended J.O.Y. plan or develop one of your own by using the guideline below. At the end of the day journal your experience on the blank lines provided.

JESUS – How you will strengthen your relationship with Jesus.

OTHERS – How you will bless and encourage Others.

YOU – How you will bless Yourself.

Remember to write the date you completed the J – O – Y!

Table Of Contents

Day 1

"You reveal the path of life to me; in your presence is abundant joy; at your right hand are eternal pleasures."

Psalm 16:11 (CSB)

The JOY Mindset

"You reveal the path of life to me; in your presence is abundant joy; at your right hand are eternal pleasures." **Psalm 16:11 (CSB)**

Most people know that JOY is one of the fruits of the spirit as listed in *Galatians 5:22*. However, few people understand its true meaning and how to apply it in their everyday lives. To experience true JOY, our mindset must be shifted from that of the world to the ultimate view of Christ.

Mindset is a set of beliefs that shape how we are influenced to make sense of the world. Having a JOY mindset is choosing to view the world through the lens of Christ where we must think, feel, and behave according to the Word.

THINK: Our thoughts should be aligned with *James 1:2*. When we experience troubles, we should get excited about the opportunity to grow.

FEEL: Our natural emotions can't be trusted, so we should remind ourselves daily of *Psalm 118:24*. Every day is the day that the Lord has made so we should choose to reJOYce and be glad in each day.

BEHAVE: *Psalm 100:1* encourages us to make a JOYful noise to the Lord. A JOY Mindset is evident when every situation, good or bad, is followed with a note of praise.

The Word of God gives the reader the blueprint to living a life full of JOY. Once we confess with our mouths and believe in our hearts that Jesus is Lord *(Romans 10:9)*, then make up our minds to follow Jesus regardless of the situation, we can experience abundant joy. Choose to have a JOY Mindset today.

Today's J.O.Y. Plan

JESUS – Study the scriptures that are mentioned in today's devotional; *Psalm 16:11, Galatians 5:22, James 1:2, Psalm 118:24, Psalm 100:1, & Romans 10:9.*

OTHERS – Share two of the scriptures you studied and why those scriptures are so important with two people.

YOU – Recall a troublesome situation that is going on around you and spend a minimum of thirty minutes praising God for the growth in the situation. The time can be broken up into 5-10 min. increments.

Date Completed ___________________________

Reflect on the Day's J.O.Y. Action Plan

Write any accomplishments, notes from study, responses from others, etc.

____

____

____

____

____

____

____

____

____

____

____

____

Day 1

About The Visionary Author

Nicole Crews Carter, The Ultimate J.O.Y. Leader, is known as the thermostat that changes the climate of any room. Her contagious smile illustrates the vision that God wants for everyone – true JOY.

Nicole is an ordained minister, award-winning speaker, author and middle school Career and Technical Education teacher with an extensive business, education, and presentation background. She spent 20 years as a leader at a Fortune 200 corporation while teaching as an adjunct professor at local community colleges. She has a bachelor's degree in Finance and a master's of Business Administration.

Nicole is married to Pastor Craig Carter who leads Shattered Chains Christian Ministry. Pastor Carter blessed her to share her Teaching gift with the ministry by facilitating Bible Study every Tuesday evening. She birthed two amazing daughters, Courtney & Mikayla. God also saw fit to grant her 7 bonus children and 11 grandchildren.

Most importantly, she loves God and thoroughly enjoys learning & teaching His word. Her upbeat storytelling teaching & coaching techniques will leave a long-lasting impression on YOU and will invoke immediate change.

Website: www.EstablishingJOY.com
Email: Info@EstablishingJOY.com
Facebook: www.facebook.com/EstablishingJOY1
Instagram: www.Instagram.com/EstablishingJOY
X (formerly Twitter): www.x.com/EstablishingJOY
YouTube: www.YouTube.com/@EstablishingJOY
LinkedIn: www.linkedin.com/in/NicoleCrewsCarter
ClubHouse: www.clubhouse.com/house/Establishing-JOY

Day 2

"Jesus replied, "You must love the LORD your God with all your heart, all your soul, and all your mind. This is the first and greatest commandment. A second is equally important: Love your neighbor as yourself"

Matthew 22:37-39 (NLT)

L.O.G.I.N

(**L**ove **O**n **G**od **I**ntentionally **N**ow)

"Jesus replied, "You must love the LORD your God with all your heart, all your soul, and all your mind. This is the first and greatest commandment. A second is equally important: Love your neighbor as yourself"
Matthew 22:37-39 (NLT)

Almost everyone has a computer or technical device that requires a login to access the files and systems needed to accomplish their work for the day. As Christ followers, we must intentionally connect with God each day in order to accomplish the work Jesus ordained and to receive instructions for the tasks ahead.

Matthew 22:37 reminds us that the first and greatest commandment is to love God with all our hearts, minds, and souls. The nataph L.O.G.I.N. (Love On God Intentionally Now), encapsulates this scripture. Love is the first step to logging in to God, and love is the first step to taking action in how we allow Him to give us instructions. When we pray, praise, worship, study the bible, obey, trust, love others, give, and serve God, we are showing God how much we love him.

Logging into your computer only to experience technical difficulties can be frustrating, right? Well, not so with God. The airwaves are never disrupted when we log in to God. God is a glitch-free God. His constant online presence is due to the fact that he doesn't sleep or take naps. We give God Joy when we login daily and according to *Psalm 22:3*, God inhabits our praise. Our obedience and love are honored by Him, and we should be Joyful about it.

Today's J.O.Y. Plan

JESUS – L.O.G.I.N. (Learn One Great Incredible Name) Study some names of God and start using them in your talks with Him. *For example, study the name Adoni.*

OTHERS – L.O.G.I.N. (Love Others Gladly & Invite a Neighbor) Invite someone to a fun activity or outing.

YOU – L.O.G.I.N. (Let Obstacles Go & Initiate New) What old habit has been an obstacle blocking your JOY? Work to let go and initiate a new, positive habit.

Date Completed ______________________

Reflect on the Day's J.O.Y. Action Plan

Write any accomplishments, notes from study, responses from others, etc.

Day 2

About The Author

Janice J. Burton, known as The Marriage Planning Mogul, is a speaker, author, event emcee, and relationship coach who shares the gospel of Jesus Christ as God gives opportunities. She is passionate about equipping singles and engaged couples to plan for marriage and is the author of "DO I?" Questions To Answer Before You Say "I DO", a marriage planning resource. Janice is the Director of Development for a nonprofit organization. She serves in ministry at Wesley United Methodist Church, Austin, TX as a bible study leader and choir member. She is a featured speaker with Christian Women Speakers and Women of Movement speaking networks. Janice is a member of Delta Sigma Theta Sorority Inc., She is a native Tennessean living in Austin, TX., has a loving son, and enjoys writing, reading, traveling, and spending time with family and friends.

Website: www.doithebook.com
Email: jjburtonenterprises@gmail.com.

Additional Notes

___

___

___

___

___

___

___

___

___

Day 3

"And the Lord went before them by day in a pillar of a cloud, to lead them the way; and by night in a pillar of fire, to give them light; to go by day and night: He took not away the pillar of the cloud by day, nor the pillar of fire by night, from before the people."

Exodus 13:21-22 (KJV 1900)

Stay In the F.O.G.
(Faith of God, Fear of God & Favor of God)

"And the Lord went before them by day in a pillar of a cloud, to lead them the way; and by night in a pillar of fire, to give them light; to go by day and night: He took not away the pillar of the cloud by day, nor the pillar of fire by night, from before the people."
Exodus 13:21-22 (KJV 1900)

The fog was so dense one morning while I was on the back screened-in porch. As I was enjoying a hot cup of coffee, I found myself feeling curious about the purpose of the fog and how it was formed. I was thinking how dangerous fog this thick is to drive in, and how glad I was that I did not have to drive anywhere that morning. Though I was not praying at that time, the Holy Spirit began to speak to me about my thoughts. The Spirit said stay in the fog. I thought what, why would anyone want to stay in the fog. It was in that moment that *Exodus 13:21-22* was brought to my remembrance.

He said again stay in the fog, but then He said something that brought me to tears. The acronym for F.O.G. stands for Faith Of God, Fear Of God and Favor Of God. He warned me that when we walk by faith, we stay in the Faith of God. We are not worried about what we do or do not see. We're totally trusting God for the next step. Fear of God is the reverence we must keep to a Holy and sovereign God. It is dangerous to lose respect for God's will and way. It is pride that causes us to move out of Faith of God, and pride comes before the fall. Lastly Remaining in Faith and Fear of God positions us to experience the Favor of God!

Think about your life and the current set of circumstances you are facing. Examine your posture. Are you walking in the Faith of God, keeping your reverence as in the Fear of God or have you decided to take another route, a shortcut or perhaps even an about-face? If yes, repent and get back into the F.O.G. It's a path that yields you to experience the Favor of God.

Today's J.O.Y. Plan

JESUS – Study the scripture Exodus 13:21-22

OTHERS – Reach out to a friend or family member that you know are in an uncertain situation and encourage them. Offer to pray with them that they stay in the Faith.

YOU – Relax, stay in the Faith by doing something relaxing today.

Date Completed ______________________

Reflect on the Day's J.O.Y. Action Plan

Write any accomplishments, notes from study, responses from others, etc.

____

____

____

____

____

____

____

____

____

____

____

____

____

____

About The Author

Danielle Suggs (The JOYful One) is a wife, birth mother of three, bonus son, and 1 grandchild. She is an Ordained Minister and is certified in Spiritual First Aid. She is a native of Upstate NY and US Army Veteran, called to intercede she is Pastor over the Prayer Ministry of The Bridge Church in Goldsboro, NC where she serves along side her husband who is the Worship Pastor. Known to her corkers as Dannie, Danielle is a Human Resources Generalist and deeply enjoys supporting the employees in many instances. Danielle often refers to herself as "The Joyful One" and has a non-profit organization "The Joyful State of Mind" that provides free services to aid those who find themselves struggling to find peace amongst the challenges of life. She is currently working on her first book due to be released later this year. Her mission and motto is "Spread Joy"

Additional Notes

___

___

___

___

___

___

___

___

___

Day 4

"For if you live according to the flesh, you will die; but if by the Spirit you put to death the misdeeds of the body, you will live." **Romans 8:13 (NIV)**

Walking in Daily Victory

"For if you live according to the flesh, you will die; but if by the Spirit you put to death the misdeeds of the body, you will live." ***Romans 8:13 (NIV)***

Christians must learn to live a life of walking in victory every day in Christ Jesus. Honoring Christ and glorifying His name should be the focus of our lives. In doing so, we gain the strength and power to overcome daily challenges and temptations.

In his letter to the Romans, the Apostle Paul wrote about the importance of walking in victory in Christ. His words remind us that we cannot live victorious lives in our own strength. We must rely on the Holy Spirit to help us overcome the sinful desires of our flesh.

In order to walk in daily victory in Christ Jesus, it is essential to stay connected to Him by praying and studying His Word. When we stay connected to Jesus, we receive and can rely on His strength and power to overcome our challenges. By walking in daily victory, we can better resist the devil and his temptations, reminding us that we are conquerors through Christ and can overcome anything we face. Let's trust in His promises and do these things so that we can live victorious lives that honor Him and bring glory to His name.

Today's J.O.Y. Plan

JESUS – Read this devotion. Study the devotion scripture and search other scriptures that align with His truth.

OTHERS – Share with at least two people you encounter today, the power they can gain by walking in victory through Christ Jesus. Share with an empowering scripture and let them know the price has already been paid for their victory.

YOU – Sit and be still for thirty minutes and reflect on how God has already brought you through and how you came out victorious.

Date Completed ___________________________

Reflect on the Day's J.O.Y. Action Plan

Write any accomplishments, notes from study, responses from others, etc.

____

____

____

____

____

____

____

____

____

____

____

About The Author

Dr. Annette West lives in Sumter, SC, with her spouse John, retired military. They have three adult children and seven grandchildren. Annette was saved in 1984 and loves God and His people. She hopes we can find the needed alignment for our mind-body-spirit, as our daily goal should be good stewards of our body and realize everything we do relates to our well-being.

She is an ordained minister, prophetic, evangelistic voice to the world, pastoral counselor, and holistic wellness life coach, sharing information, products, and services that have helped her through her journey.

She is the CEO of JATNE Publishing, offering writing, publishing, branding, marketing, and book launch services. Also, she is a self-published author of several books and hundreds of devotionals and studies. She has a doctorate in Business Administration with an emphasis in Management, Human Resources, and International Business Relations.

She is active in prison ministry and works logistically with the Victorious Golgotha Mission School in Kakamega, Kenya.

Let us not just hear the word only but live to please the Lord.
(James 1:22)

Website: www.JATNEpublishing.org
Email: Jatnepublishing@gmail.com
Facebook Group: JATNE Publishing

Additional Notes

___

___

___

Day 5

"For we are His workmanship [His own master work, a work of art], created in Christ Jesus [reborn from above—spiritually transformed, renewed, ready to be used] for good works, which God prepared [for us] beforehand [taking paths which He set], so that we would walk in them [living the good life which He prearranged and made ready for us]." **Ephesians 2:20 (AMP)**

I AM PURPOSE!

"For we are His workmanship [His own master work, a work of art], created in Christ Jesus [reborn from above—spiritually transformed, renewed, ready to be used] for good works, which God prepared [for us] beforehand [taking paths which He set], so that we would walk in them [living the good life which He prearranged and made ready for us]."
Ephesians 2:20 (AMP)

In the beginning, God blew Rua breath from the dust and made me, a masterpiece unto his own likeness and image. He knew me before He formed and placed me in the womb of my mother. Because of the plans God had for me, He predestined my story: Abandoned but Anointed. Adopted but not Aborted. Abused but Survived. Imprisoned but Set Free. Lost but Found. Victim but not Vindictive. What's the story that God has predestined for you?

We are a workmanship reborn, transformed, renewed, ready to do good works that God prepared beforehand for us to walk in. Who but God would have ever known? Have you ever had a retrospect snapshot moment of your life? A lightning flash of where God has brought you from. It doesn't matter if you are walking into, going thru, still standing, or overcame to come out of your storm(situation); God knew He could trust you to handle it. So, trust Him (totally rely upon the Savior today) with His promise in *Jeremiah 29:11*. He knew you would be the one who would purposely testify, capture, and draw souls to fall in love with him. Can you still hear the sound? The echoing promise of God saying, "BE (believe & expect) still and know, that I AM God? *Psalm 46:10*

Remember, "He did it before, and He will do it again. Same God yesterday, today, and forever more. *Hebrews 13:8*. Well, that's my moment as you are reading this devotion. I am starting to live with purpose all over again. Our God is a God of fresh starts and new beginnings. From the morning sunrise to the changing seasons, to the passing years.

Day 5

I went through the 'Stripping Storm' (covid, deaths, ministry alignment, divorce, financial hardships) along with the 2022 S.A.C.H.E.T. (sarcasm, abuse, criticism, hypocrites, embarrassment, trials & tribulations). B.U.T. (better understand this), God knew my purpose would not be thwarted *(Job 42:2)*. God already knew the plans of his handiwork for ME. They were created through Christ Jesus as good works that HE prepared in advance for ME to do. He did it for me and yes, He is awaiting to do it for you.

Today's J.O.Y. Plan

JESUS – Know who you are to God. Study *Romans 8: 29-30, Job 42:2; Ephesians 2:20*

OTHERS - Give love in action (word, deed, or gesture) everywhere you go today. The marketplace isn't ready for 'straight transparent' ministry, yet the 'straight transparent' ministry should be ready for the marketplace. *Acts 20:24*.

YOU - Celebrate the moment. You made it. You did it. Reward yourself. Have a Me day on purpose (intentionally).

Date Completed ______________________

Reflect on the Day's J.O.Y. Action Plan

Write any accomplishments, notes from study, responses from others, etc.

____

____

____

____

____

____

____

____

____

____

____

____

Dr. Cindy Betts formerly Bailey, a born-again believer of Jesus Christ, bold about Kingdom business, and a fearless Prayer Warrior & Intercessor for God's People. She is a native of Port-of-Spain, Trinidad, Cuban & African/American descent.

She's a King's kid, a Queen, a Mother, a Grandmother, and a Great-grandmother. Cindy holds several additional titles where she serves as an International Evangelist, Teacher, Certified Life Coach, Wealth Coach, Radio Host, Author, Motivational and Leadership Speaker, Law Enforcement Counselor, Chaplin, Global Entrepreneur, Lecturer, Director of Operations, Financial Specialist, Certified Tax Preparer, Ordained Minister, K I N International Ministry Inc. Founder, and member of multiple corporate and non-profit boards.

Dr. Cindy holds an Associates Degree in Accounting and Banking Operations, Bachelors Degree in Finance, Masters Degree in Psychology and Family Counseling, Masters and Doctorate of Divinity in Christian Counseling.

She is the surviving founder of Sisters of Freedom House Foundation in Ghana, Accra for orphans and widows. She has traveled 23 countries and 40 states consulting and coaching wealth to build empires.

As a philanthropic 'Ambassador for Christ', she lives her favorite scripture located in *Matthew 6:33 (AMP)*

Website: www.KINinternationalministry.org
Email: IhaveKingdomPurpose@gmail.com

Additional Notes

____

____

____

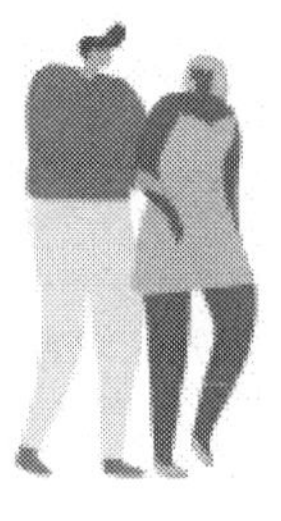

Day 6

"But He has said to me, "My grace is sufficient for you [My loving kindness and My mercy are more than enough—always available—regardless of the situation; for [My] power is being perfected [and is completed and shows itself most effectively] in [your] weakness. "Therefore, I will all the more gladly boast in my weaknesses, so that the power of Christ [may completely enfold me and] may dwell in me"

2 Corinthians 12:9 (AMP)

Weak

"But He has said to me, "My grace is sufficient for you [My loving kindness and My mercy are more than enough—always available—regardless of the situation; for [My] power is being perfected [and is completed and shows itself most effectively] in [your] weakness. "Therefore, I will all the more gladly boast in my weaknesses, so that the power of Christ [may completely enfold me and] may dwell in me"
2 Corinthians 12:9 (AMP)

It was the first day of a new month, and I was excited to climb out of bed to start my day. I put on my two prosthetic legs and *attempted* to transfer from my bed to my wheelchair. Attempted is the key word here as the brakes on my wheelchair malfunctioned, and I fell straight to the floor. BAM! Because I am a bilateral below-knee amputee, my beautiful wife had to call the paramedics to get me up off of the floor. See, I have not mastered the art of getting myself off the floor under my own strength. Let's face it, since my health issues, I am physically weak. It is just a fact.

I have always associated weakness with negativity. *"His game is weak"*, *"his rap is weak"*, or *"get that weak stuff out of here"*. Many of you may feel weak as well. The good news is that we are not alone as the Bible is filled with "weak" people that God was able to perfect.

When God revealed himself to Moses in a burning bush and asked him to lead His people out of Egypt, Moses said that he couldn't do it because he stuttered. Weak! Still, with Pharaoh in hot pursuit, and the Red Sea as a roadblock, he marched his people towards the promised land. Elijah, a great profit who could also fall into the Weak category after winning a great victory for the Lord at Mount Carmel, and then ran from Jezebel, laid under a tree, ate a snack, and cried himself to

sleep. Peter denied knowing Christ three times and cried bitterly afterwards. Weak! David had Uriah's wife. WEAK! Sampson had Delilah. Weak! Yet they are all remembered as heroes in the Bible.

If you are feeling physically, spiritually, or emotionally weak, God may have you exactly where he wants you. God is not caught off guard by our shortcomings and He has a long record of exchanging our weaknesses for HIS strength.

Today's J.O.Y. Plan

JESUS - Reflect on two translations of 2 Corinthians 12:9.

OTHERS - Pray for a friend that has a physical, mental, emotional, or spiritual weakness. Offer to be an accountability partner.

YOU - Confess your weaknesses to God and commit to taking an action to be 1% better today.

Date Completed ______________________

Reflect on the Day's J.O.Y. Action Plan

Write any accomplishments, notes from study, responses from others, etc.

____

____

____

____

____

____

____

____

____

____

____

____

Day 6

About The Author

As a customer journey executive for 20 years, Elder Darren "DC" Lyons built relationships across the globe, managing a business process outsourcer organization in Asia, Central America and South America. When he was the director of global customer care for 1-800-flowers.com, he led a vendor organization of 1000 FTE across seven partners in five countries and ten cities. Over the past five years, Darren has had numerous health issues, including two below-knee amputations, stage five kidney failure requiring dialysis three times a week, and he is a stroke survivor.

Darren is a member of Voice of Hope Seventh Day Adventist Church where he serves as an Elder, a member of the Finance Committee and the committee on Disabilities.

He obtained his Bachelors degree in History from George Mason University and Masters Degree in Organizational Management from the University of Phoenix. Darren and his lovely wife Elaine founded Korrior, Inc. with a vision to create inspirational books and faith-based media projects. Darren's book "With Worn Out Tools: Navigating the Rituals of Midlife" was released in September 2019.

He is an Executive Coach, Trainer and Keynote Speaker.

Website: www.Korrior.com
Email: DcLyons@Korrior.com
Instagram: www.Instagram.com/korrior

Additional Notes

____

____

____

____

____

Day 7

"Look up and see! Who created these? He brings out the stars by number; he calls all of them by name. Because of his great power and strength, not one of them is missing." **Isaiah 40:26 (CSB)**

Look Up Child

"Look up and see! Who created these? He brings out the stars by number; he calls all of them by name. Because of his great power and strength, not one of them is missing." ***Isaiah 40:26 (CSB)***

How often do you stop and look around? I mean really look around to take in your surroundings like the landscape, or the people coming or going? If you are like many, you may keep on with the tasks and responsibilities of your day and at the end of the day, you have simply gone through the motions, never truly stopping to look or see beyond what is right in front of you.

To look up requires you to take in what is around you, and I love how scripture commands us to "look up and see." Our vision becomes clearer when we take our gaze away from our own tasks to take in another's perspective and then look even higher towards God's perspective on our daily life.

As someone living away from bright lights and big cities, my country skies are filled to the brim with stars, and even the Milky Way galaxy I see is just a small glimpse into the fullness of the universe, yet our God knows and calls every star by name.

You can trust that the God who created and sustains the stars with His power and strength also knows you intimately and by name. The same God who created the universe created you and will uphold you in all things. You do not need to rely on your own power and strength. You need only to "look up and see."

Today's J.O.Y. Plan

JESUS - Listen to Lauren Daigle's "Look Up Child" and meditate on *Isaiah Chapter 40.*

OTHERS - Look up and out for the stranger in your midst. Offer a warm greeting to five strangers on your path today or pray to see those in your midst that you do not normally pay attention to or care for and show them Christ's love.

YOU - Take fifteen minutes from your day or evening to stop, breathe, and look to the sky, the hills, or the horizon to consider the works and wonders of creation as you stretch, breathe, pray, or praise.

Date Completed ______________________________

Reflect on the Day's J.O.Y. Action Plan

Write any accomplishments, notes from study, responses from others, etc.

____

____

____

____

____

____

____

____

____

____

____

____

About The Author

Michele Baran is an Upstate New York native and Finger Lakes Region enthusiast. She is currently navigating midlife, work, and faith with intentionality and spontaneity. Her best work aims to both simplify complexities and expand possibilities around career, passion, And life design at Life Design Solutions, LLC.

She holds undergraduate and graduate degrees in education from State University of New York (SUNY) Cortland.

Michele married her high school sweetheart who is an extreme athlete and artist. They raised two wonderful young adults in the hills of the Finger Lakes.

LinkedIn: www.Linkedin.com/in/michelebaran

Additional Notes

"For we know, brothers and sisters loved by God, that he has chosen you."

1 Thessalonians 1:4 (NIV)

Chasing Dreams

"For we know, brothers and sisters loved by God, that he has chosen you." ***1 Thessalonians 1:4 (NIV)***

How often do we hear the terms: Live Your Dreams, Dream Big, Dream Chasers, Chase your Dreams, etc. All these phrases are positive affirmations and can easily empower a person to pursue their dreams, but you will find that God chooses you to fulfill the dream that He placed inside of you purposefully. Just like he did David who was minding his own business herding sheep. God knew that He called David to be the next King of Israel and David had to fulfill that dream because he was chosen for the assignment.

I saw Chasing Dreams in a different light when my son passed away in 2022. His Dreams were to become an Aspiring Rap Artist, but he never got a chance to see his dreams become a reality. Did God choose his dream or was his dream his own and pursuing it became a chase for things that were not chosen for him by God. I supported his dream but I was not fond of what he desired to do with his life, so I showed up with the why behind my dislike in subtle ways since I had already given him a foundation of who God was. There was guilt in my decision for being too delicate, so I covered that guilt by presenting him with a bible that had the following message: *Dearest Son, this bible is presented to you as a guide and blueprint for your life. If you want wisdom, Proverbs and James are great chapters that will teach you how to live with integrity (doing the right thing). Also, the book of Psalms is full of great prayers and if you want to know more about Jesus, read the New Testament. This is my gift to you because you are my gift from God. I pray that you are blessed abundantly in every area of your life. Love You, Mom.*

God will equip you (sometimes supernaturally) for the dream He chooses for you. Rather you pursue a desire that urges at

you constantly, run away from one that scares you, or end up in a role that only God could have gotten you in, He will allow trials and tribulations in your life until the dream you're pursuing is accomplished according to His plan, His will, His purpose, His glory.

The dream that God has for you is far greater than any dream you're dreaming for yourself because it's the gift and/or talents that He instills inside of you to fulfill the purpose that He has for your life.

Today's J.O.Y. Plan

JESUS – Chase your Dreams to fulfill God's purpose for your life by meditating on this scripture, *Hebrews 13:20-21.*

OTHERS – Encourage a loved one to understand that dreams are God's purposeful fulfillment in their lives specifically chosen for them and share *Proverbs 18:16* with them.

YOU – Dream BIG and know that there will be no obstacle that can stand in the way of what God has gifted you.

Date Completed ____________________________

Reflect on the Day's J.O.Y. Action Plan

Write any accomplishments, notes from study, responses from others, etc.

____

____

____

____

____

____

____

____

____

____

____

____

About The Author

Jacqueline Thompson is first, a storyteller of Life with stories that are heartfelt, authentic, and genuinely written to touch the readers she speaks to! Her experiences, situations, and circumstances are impactful to the woman she continues to evolve into today, tomorrow, and forever more. Her life journey is purpose-driven and she holds nothing back in sharing her experiences so that others can embrace life knowing that they are not alone. A Chicago native who now resides in Atlanta, GA credits her gift of storytelling to God, her children, and the little people in her life who call her MiMi!

A Dual Certified Life Coach with a B.O.S.S. (Being One Smart Sister) status approach who empowers aspiring, new, and seasoned Authors to value how life experiences and learned lessons translate into captivating words that come to life, creating a powerful message to impact the lives of others! Additionally, Jacqueline helps emerging career-minded individuals uncover what's holding them back from being totally equipped to boldly walk in their God-given purpose by maximizing life skills with Godly principles along their journey to destination Greatness in their careers and businesses.

Jacqueline is also the owner of Penned Just Write, LLC which specializes in publishing Storytellers who desire to bring their voice to life from start to finish!!! Connect with Coach Jacqueline on these social media platforms:

Website: www.pennedjustwrite.com
Instagram: www.Instagram/justcoachjacqueline
Facebook: www.facebook.com/justcoachjacqueline

Additional Notes

____

____

____

____

Day 9

"For we are His workmanship, created in Christ Jesus for good works, which God prepared beforehand that we should walk in them."

Ephesians 2:10 (ESV)

My Identity – Who are YOU in Christ?

"For we are His workmanship, created in Christ Jesus for good works, which God prepared beforehand that we should walk in them."
Ephesians 2:10 (ESV)

Having a sense of identity is important because it allows people to stand out as individuals and develop a sense of well-being. Humans express a sense of identity verbally and nonverbally by the way we talk, our social status, and even our race. Identity is the unique set of characteristics that is used to identify a person as themselves and no one else. But, on a personal level, identity can refer to a person's sense of self, meaning how they view them as compared to other people.

Learning who you are as a child can make a difference in WHO YOU ARE as you mature in life. Growing up in my parents' home, there were four girls and two boys. Being one of the first two siblings and a twin was always a joy for me, and seeing twins today still fascinates me. Although twins are born at the same time, they have their own DNA and their own name. As we matured and developed our own sense of identity, I (Eileen) was known as the *outspoken* twin and Arleen was known as the *soft-spoken* twin. Sometimes people would say to me, "Why aren't you like your sister? She's quiet and easygoing." The comments would go on and sometimes it made me feel some kind of way. "We're twins but we are different", I thought.

As I matured in Christ, I discovered that I am a child of the most high God. I am made in His image and created in Him to do good works of which He knew in advance. I am fearfully and wonderfully made. Be OK with others speaking their minds but be identified by whom God says you are. I am a worshipper, one who praises, an encourager, excepted and I am chosen. I am God's masterpiece, free to be me and that's what He sees. Who are you in Christ?

Today's J.O.Y. Plan

JESUS – Read scriptures on Identity to discover who you are in Christ.

OTHERS – Encourage someone by writing out the meaning of their name and giving it to them.

YOU – Affirmation: I AM CONFIDENT OF WHO I AM! (repeat this verbally every hour today)

Date Completed ____________________________

Reflect on the Day's J.O.Y. Action Plan

Write any accomplishments, notes from study, responses from others, etc.

____

____

____

____

____

____

____

____

____

____

____

____

____

Day 9

About The Author

Minister Eileen Tarpley Williams is a native of Axton, VA. She attended Pittsylvania County Schools and graduated from Danville Community College. She also graduated June 2016 from North Carolina Theological University, Thomasville, NC with an Associates Degree in Biblical Studies. She is currently employed by CATO Fashions as an Assistant Store Manager.

She has been married to her husband Ronnie for 42 years. They have one married daughter Erica (Thomas) and one granddaughter Kynzlie.

She was called into the ministry and preached her first sermon on August 17, 2013, at Tarpley Chapel Baptist Church. What price will you pay to be a servant of God and to serve His people? She received her license under the leadership of Pastor Robert L. Divens, Jr. Praise & Worship is who she is and loves to make a joyful noise. She is an advocate of Women and believes they should always wear CONFIDENCE. It does not matter the race, culture or denomination, women are "Designed to Influence" other women. She is a Certified Financial Coach and speaks to people so they can develop a better relationship with their wealth.

Email: Designed4influence@yahoo.com
Facebook: www.facebook.com/eileentarpleywilliams
Instagram: www.instagram.com/Eileentw1
Linkedin: www.Linkedin.com/in/EileenTWilliams

Additional Notes

____

____

____

____

____

Day 10

"If anyone among you thinks he is religious and does not bridle his tongue but deceives his own heart, this one's religion is useless."

James 1:26 (NKJV)

Day 10

Accepted and Loved by Him

"If anyone among you thinks he is religious and does not bridle his tongue but deceives his own heart, this one's religion is useless."
James 1:26 (NKJV)

I was raised in a household where feelings were not spoken about. There was domestic violence, and no one was allowed to discuss it or allow the "outside" world to know. We looked like the perfect American family, but little did anyone know the horrors that were happening inside our home. This trauma had a very negative effect on me. I repressed things until I was eighteen and all of a sudden, it came flooding back. Can you imagine how I lived my life during that blocked-out stage? Let's say it was less than stellar. Once I was on my own, I felt free to express myself in any way that I saw fit. If you hurt me, you were going to know about it. My emotions ran rapidly and in turn, destroyed my already bruised mental state and nervous system as if it wasn't already fragile. It is only in this time of surrendering to God that I realize that emotions are just that. Nothing more and we do not have to be ruled by them.

I am working very hard at learning how to control my emotions, which is something I was never taught as a child. Your feelings were to be stuffed down. You were to be seen and not heard. There was a lot of physical, verbal, emotional, and sexual violence in my life as a child but God Has shown me that I am *Accepted and Loved by Him*.

Surrendering to God every day has been a great help to my emotional well-being. The lessons learned are hard but necessary. What's important to me today are my methods of breathing exercises, movement, scripture, and understanding the importance of setting boundaries. Who would have known that a woman of little self-esteem could set boundaries? Not me but what I know to be true is that setting boundaries and not honoring them is where the real work comes into play. This new dedication toward transformation is scary but beautiful at the same time. Don't allow your emotions to rule your life and know that You are *Accepted and Loved by Him*. You can do it!

Day 10

Today's J.O.Y. Plan

JESUS – Sit in silence and talk to Jesus about your sufferings. Ask him to rebuke any negative ties on your soul because of what you have been through. Read *James 1.*

OTHERS – Reach out to someone whom you don't have patience for and show them love today. Before you do it, practice how you will speak to them and exercise control over your emotions.

YOU – Write a list of all the ways you will begin to practice controlling some of your negative emotions. After making the list, do something fun for yourself that doesn't cost anything.

Date Completed ______________________________

Reflect on the Day's J.O.Y. Action Plan

Write any accomplishments, notes from study, responses from others, etc.

____

____

____

____

____

____

____

____

____

____

____

Day 10

About The Author

Elisa Daguanno was born and raised in Long Island, NY. She was blessed to be ushered by an innate creative mind. She studied to be an opera singer only because pop music wasn't an option at the college she attended. Her beautiful voice led her to sing in a wedding band for six years. Currently she is an educator in the New York City Public School system.

Unfortunately, Elisa grew up in a domestically violent home which caused her to make poor decisions throughout her adult life. She studied yoga which allowed her to work on her emotional intelligence that gave her the strength to lead her out of a domestically violent marriage. With God's help, she is on a quest to heal her traumatic upbringing and poor life choices. Her dream is to own a brick-and-mortar cafe with a yoga studio and mental health clinic that will host entertaining and informational classes at night. Elisa looks forward to working with women to help them see their value and potential.

In addition to her two children that she loves, her passion is her luxury custom crochet business called Yarn Art!

Instagram: www.instagram.com/yarn_art
Facebook: www.facebook.com/elisasyarnboutique

Additional Notes

____

____

____

____

____

____

____

Day 11

"He that dwelleth in the secret place of the most High shall abide under the shadow of the Almighty."

Psalms 91:1 (KJV)

Shadow of the Almighty

"He that dwelleth in the secret place of the most High shall abide under the shadow of the Almighty." **Psalms 91:1 (KJV)**

To dwell in the shadow of the Almighty is to live under the promise of God's protection. The theme of *Psalm 91* focuses a spotlight on absolute trust in God and loyalty to Him. This kind of trust suggests intimate friendship with God. It is this sort of loving relationship that inspires the psalmist to say, *"How precious is your steadfast love, O God! The children of mankind take refuge in the shadow of your wings" (Psalm 36:7-8 ESV).* It is the attitude of one who clings to the Lord at all times, saying, *"For he will hide me in his shelter in the day of trouble; he will conceal me under the cover of his tent; he will lift me high upon a rock" (Psalm 27:5 ESV)*

Psalm 91:9-14 (NLT) continues, *"If you make the LORD your refuge, if you make the Most High your shelter, no evil will conquer you; no plague will come near your home. For he will order his angels to protect you wherever you go. They will hold you up with their hands, so you won't even hurt your foot on a stone. You will trample upon lions and cobras; you will crush fierce lions and serpents under your feet! The LORD says, 'I will rescue those who love me. I will protect those who trust in my name."*

Abiding in God's presence, we find security, protection, and care. The ultimate victory is ours in Christ as the Almighty's shadow follows us all the days of our lives.

Today's J.O.Y. Plan

JESUS – Study *Psalm 91* and learn how to stay under the shadow of the Almighty, to gain strength and power of God.

OTHERS – Find two people today that have a need that you can help with and share with them what you learned from *Psalm 91*.

YOU- Love on yourself by writing down why understanding *Psalm 91* is so important.

Date Completed ______________________________

Reflect on the Day's J.O.Y. Action Plan

Write any accomplishments, notes from study, responses from others, etc.

____

____

____

____

____

____

____

____

____

____

____

____

____

Day 11

About The Author

Elder Sylvester Durham was born in Detroit, Michigan on January 11, to the late Calvin Durham III and Margaret Foster Durham. At an early age he attended New Bethel Baptist Church under the leadership of C. L. Franklin. He was very active in church, serving as a music director and song leader.

After moving from Detroit Michigan to Martinsville Virginia, Sylvester was filled with the Holy Spirit and began worshiping with Dr. Lettie P. Cohen in Axton Virginia. He pursued his education while serving as an armor bearer, usher, missionary, and choir member. He was licensed as a minister by the United Holy Church of America in 1988 and received his Doctor of Divinity in 2022 from Living Epistle Bible College 2.0.

Sylvester met the love of his life, Stella Marie Baize, while serving at Gospel Light United Holy Church. The Lord blessed them with one son, Cameron Sylvester Durham and one grandchild.

His favorite scripture is *Psalms 91:1*. He loves to eat his Aunt Clarice's pinto beans and his cousin Margaret's banana pudding.

Additional Notes

____

____

____

____

____

____

____

Day 12

"For we walk by faith, not by sight." ***2 Corinthians 5:7 (KJV)***

Day 12

Close Your Eyes in the Dark

"For we walk by faith, not by sight." **2 Corinthians 5:7 (KJV)**

It isn't a matter of if the darkness will come, but rather when. I want you to think about a current or upcoming situation that is dark. Can you dare to close your eyes in the dark? This question or statement is oxymoronic at best. It is in the dark when we naturally open our eyes as wide as we can to allow light into our eyes to help us see. Spiritually, we close our eyes and walk by faith not by sight.

Last week I entered my dark bedroom and clicked the light switch on the wall. The bulb was blown. But no problem, right? On the other side of the room is another light. My room was dimly lit from the back porch light. The other light switch is just beyond the dresser, so I focused on it.

As I focused on this dresser and started to walk, I bumped my right leg on the footboard of the bed. Hopping on my left leg, I tripped on a pair of shoes I'd left at the end of the bed. *Ouch*, I murmured. While sitting on the floor, I heard the Spirit of God say, "close your eyes." After I gathered myself, I stood up, closed my eyes, and began to feel my way to the dresser. Sure enough, at the end of the dresser was the light switch. Standing there, I understood the message God gave me in closing my eyes in the dark.

I want to encourage you today to have faith in God during the darkest times of your life. Walk by faith, not by sight. You shouldn't let dimly lit objects in your view distract you. For instance, I was able to focus on my goal, the dresser, with the help of the artificial light from my back porch. But, because my focus was distorted in the artificial light, I didn't see the obstacles along the way.

Situations in life tend to cast darkness. It may be a doctor's report, the loss of a job, the end of a relationship, or maybe the death of a loved one. We have victory in the dark knowing that the light of Christ will lead the way.

Jesus said: "I am the world's light. No one who follows me stumbles around in the darkness. I provide plenty of light to live in." *John 8:12 MSG*. Can you dare to Close your Eyes in the Dark?

Today's J.O.Y. Plan

JESUS - Read *John 8:12* and meditate on Jesus being the light in your dark places.

OTHERS - Share *2 Corinthians 5:7* and *John 8:12* with someone you know that is in "addiction darkness".

YOU - Spend as much time as you can in the natural sunlight today. Sit on your porch or take a walk in your neighborhood. Feel the light and love of God's Son, Jesus through his created Sun, light.

Prayer: Father, thank you for declaring light in the void known as darkness. You have consistently been the light in dark places. Thank you! You loved us to the extent of sending your darling Son, Jesus the Christ to pardon our sins. He declared he is the light of the world and we who follow him will not stumble in darkness. Amen.

Date Completed ____________________________

Reflect on the Day's J.O.Y. Action Plan

Write any accomplishments, notes from study, responses from others, etc.

____

____

____

____

____

____

____

____

About The Author

Minister Neva Brooks has combined her commitment to the calling from Christ, with her experience and expertise in mental wellness. She serves as founder and lead facilitator of "Comfort Companions," a program that teaches and establishes Mental Wellness Ministries in the Church. Her assignment is to glorify God and edify his Kingdom!

She is licensed and ordained as a minister in the Christian Faith and attends Anderson Zion Baptist Church in Anderson, Indiana. The Pastor is Cecil Golder III. God has allowed her to speak and witness on Global platforms.

As a Certified Life Coach and Registered Nurse, she spends time using her life experiences and professional career to help women who feel stuck. We navigate from the conflicts of life to places of confidence, freedom, and clarity. She does this best with nurses, in her words "I'm a nurse, I get it.!" Neva is the CEO of Diamond Sharp Coaching, LLC. and founder of Diamonds Sharpens Diamonds, a women's ministry based on the biblical principles in *Proverbs 27:17*.

Neva received nursing degrees from Anderson University and IUPUI Indianapolis. She earned a Master of Business Administration from Indiana Wesleyan University. She holds Certifications in various areas of Psychology, Mental Wellness and Behavioral Health.

She is Mother, Nana, Sister, Daughter, and true Sister-Friend, who loves her family.

Website: www.DiamondSharpCoach.com
Email: DiamonSharpCoach@gmail.com

Additional Notes

____

____

____

Day 13

"Whoever can be trusted with very little can also be trusted with much, and whoever is dishonest with very little will also be dishonest with much."

Luke 16:10 (NIV)

Day 13

Living Life in Truth

"Whoever can be trusted with very little can also be trusted with much, and whoever is dishonest with very little will also be dishonest with much." **Luke 16:10 (NIV)**

Today was a good day. I got the job! But more important, I'm walking in truth. After sixteen years of being a stay-at-home mom with five girls and twin boys, working from home (several businesses) and starting my own business, the truth finally hit me. I was only existing.

Most people who have developed a real relationship with the Lord can look back on their past and realize that their lives have been lived dishonestly. In fact, some Christians have stated that they weren't saved for real until later in life. Their former life of being in the church was about pleasing others or doing what they thought they were supposed to do. All the while they were living a lie.

God requires us to be *honest* and *trustworthy*. These two words have different meanings, but they go hand in hand. Honest means a person has the regard to tell the truth whereas a trustworthy person is reliable or deserving of one's trust.

No matter what you do, you must be true to yourself no matter what anyone else thinks or how it looks to them. By walking in His light and living accordingly, you are living the truth that is within.

Start living your life of truth today by focusing on the Word of God then living how God desires you to live.

Today's J.O.Y. Plan

JESUS – Take time to invest in His Word by studying *Luke 16.*

OTHERS – Contact the closest and the furthest person you know via call, text, or visit and tell them what's on your heart about the JOYfulness of the Lord.

YOU – Write down your honest thoughts in a journal, light a candle, and sing a song of praise.

Date Completed ___________________________

Reflect on the Day's J.O.Y. Action Plan

Write any accomplishments, notes from study, responses from others, etc.

____

____

____

____

____

____

____

____

____

____

____

____

____

Day 13

About The Author

Yolanda Coleman Brown was born in Washington and has been in Southern Maryland the last 25-years raising her blended family of five girls and twin boys. She grew up Baptist; however, the last 15-years she has attended Non-Denominational ministries.

She has served as Sunday School Director, Young adult President, in the audio ministry, and always as a student. Growing in God's word by studying and writing in journals is one of her many passions.

Yolanda is proud to be "under construction" because she realizes with God the best is yet to come!

Additional Notes

___

___

___

___

___

___

___

___

___

___

___

___

___

Day 14

"For God so loved the world, that He gave His only begotten Son, that whosoever believeth in him should not perish but have eternal life."

John 3:16(KJV)

Don’t Say Die

“For God so loved the world, that He gave His only begotten Son, that whosoever believeth in him should not perish but have eternal life.”
John 3:16(KJV)

It has always bothered me when people would say someone died. Immediately after they say it, I would respond, "Don't say die, say passed away." The word die seems so harsh and final. For years I really didn’t know why I felt so passionate about it until I began to reflect on the first scripture that I memorized above: *John 3:16 KJV.*

I could quote the King James Version of the scripture with ease. The truth behind why I didn't like the word die came to light once I broke down the scripture.

God loves us (His children) so much that He came to the world in flesh in order to be treated brutally so that we will never have to die. There are many people who have left their earthly bodies and that is why I call it passed away. BUT they didn’t die based on *John 3:16.* We can’t die if we believe in Him. If we truly believe, and develop a real relationship with Jesus, we will have live forever.

Don't say die, but rather remember *John 3:16*.

Today's J.O.Y. Plan

JESUS – Study *John 3* and write out the role of Jesus as our Savior.

OTHERS – Text the most important thing you learned in *John 3* to three random contacts in your phone.

YOU – Love on yourself today by doing one thing that you have said you didn't have time to do.

Date Completed ____________________________

Reflect on the Day's J.O.Y. Action Plan

Write any accomplishments, notes from study, responses from others, etc.

____

____

____

____

____

____

____

____

____

____

____

____

____

Day 14

About The Author

Mikayla Penn is the youngest daughter of Nicole (Craig) Carter & Donnie Penn. She has a heart of gold and is known for her loyalty, compassion, athleticism, and jovial character. She was raised in the Baptist church, singing in the choir & playing the drums.

During High School, she was a leader on the basketball court (point guard) and on the drumline (playing all drum types). Volunteering is a passion of hers, especially with the Special Olympics. She believes in the "One Band, One Sound" on the field, the court, and with those with special needs.

Mikayla is currently sharing her skills in the hospitality industry as a leader in customer service.

Additional Notes

____

____

____

____

____

____

____

____

____

____

____

____

____

Day 15

"Have you not known? Have you not heard? The LORD is the everlasting God, the Creator of the ends of the earth. He does not faint or grow weary; his understanding is unsearchable. He gives power to the faint, and to him who has no might he increases strength. Even youths shall faint and be weary, and young men shall fall exhausted; but they who wait for the LORD shall renew their strength; they shall mount up with wings like eagles; they shall run and not be weary; they shall walk and not faint.

Isaiah 40:28-31 (ESV)

You're BIGGER

"Have you not known? Have you not heard? The LORD is the everlasting God, the Creator of the ends of the earth. He does not faint or grow weary; his understanding is unsearchable. He gives power to the faint, and to him who has no might he increases strength. Even youths shall faint and be weary, and young men shall fall exhausted; but they who wait for the LORD shall renew their strength; they shall mount up with wings like eagles; they shall run and not be weary; they shall walk and not faint. ***Isaiah 40:28-31 (ESV)***

Jekalyn Carr has a song called "You're Bigger". There are two lines in the song that speak directly to my heart, and they are "You're bigger than the problems that I've faced" and "You're bigger than the disasters I've seen". The song is stating that God is bigger than any problems or tragedies that life may bring, which is not only very true, but proven in God's Holy Word.

Throughout our lives, we may encounter disappointments, trials, and challenges such as arguments, loss of employment, divorce, or health issues. No matter what life may bring in the form of adversity, we serve a mighty God that will bring us through any storm. In *Jeremiah 29:11*, God tells us that He knows the plans that he has for us, plans to prosper us, and not harm us, plans to give us hope and a future. That scripture is proof that God loves us and doesn't want to harm us, which means that God even uses our problems to prosper us.

In the words of my grandmother, she would say that no trial is without a blessing and a lesson. Because of God's unconditional love for us and His Omnipotence, you can face any trial with total faith that a blessing will follow.

Today's J.O.Y. Plan

JESUS - Study *Ephesians 3:20-21 ESV*. (Also study any cross references to those verses that your Bible offers.

OTHERS - Encourage others by giving them examples of how God proved Himself to be BIGGER than problems you've faced.

YOU – Remind yourself that if God showed up for you the last time and the countless times before that, He will most certainly show up for you again. Now smile, lift up holy hands in praise and repeat as often as needed.

Date Completed ____________________________

Reflect on the Day's J.O.Y. Action Plan

Write any accomplishments, notes from study, responses from others, etc.

____

____

____

____

____

____

____

____

____

____

____

____

____

Day 15

About The Author

Leigh Harold was born and raised in Philadelphia, PA also known as "Philly", the City of Brotherly Love. She is a Woman of God on a mission to fulfill her true purpose on this earth and use every one of my God-given gifts to Glorify and Honor Him.

She is a proud mom and mom-mom (grandmother) who is determined to set high standards for future generations and to leave a legacy that will make God say, "well done, my good and faithful servant".

Currently, Leigh is a Client Services Supervisor and an entrepreneur striving to achieve at least eight streams of income.

Additional Notes

Day 16

"Faith is the substance of things hoped for the evidence of things NOT SEEN"
Hebrews 11:1 (NKJV)

Finding Your Faith In the Dark

"Faith is the substance of things hoped for the evidence of things NOT SEEN" **Hebrews 11:1 (NKJV)**

The context of *Hebrews 11:1* is not a definition of faith. It's a description of what faith does. Substance means "essence" or "reality". Faith treats things hoped for as reality. Evidence means "proof" or "conviction." Faith itself proves that what is unseen is real such as the believer's rewards at the return of Christ.

How do we measure the type of faith we really possess, especially when we find ourselves encountering so many dark places in life? These places will have us questioning our confession in Christ and challenge the very faith we say we have in Him by consuming our thoughts. We battle the darkness of depression and anxiety. We war against loneliness and self-worth and for many, the list goes on and on. Despite these challenges, we find ourselves in the writer of the scripture who gives us a fresh perspective. Faith is found in the *unseen*; it is built in the dark places we don't know how to escape. It is in these places He says, "come to him all that labor and are heavy laden and he will give us rest." Take his yoke upon us and learn of him for he is meek and lowly in heart: and we shall find rest for our souls." So, I encourage us today to look at our dark places just a little differently, and instead of being consumed by them, let us choose to find our faith in them.

Today's J.O.Y. Plan

JESUS – Meditate on Hebrews 11:1 and other scriptures on faith building

OTHERS – Pray with someone else you know is going through a dark place and help them find faith in the dark

YOU – Take some time today to do something you have been putting off just for you.

Date Completed ______________________________

Reflect on the Day's J.O.Y. Action Plan

Write any accomplishments, notes from study, responses from others, etc.

____

____

____

____

____

____

____

____

____

____

____

____

____

Day 16

About The Author

Pastor Christopher A. Campbell Sr. was born and raised in Dayton, Ohio in the Five Oaks community. He attended Dayton Public Schools and is a graduate of Colonel White High School. He went on to pursue an education at Wilmington College and earned a Bachelor of Science Degree in Human Services and Theology.

In 2007, he accepted his call to ministry. Recognizing and nurturing the anointing and calling upon his life, he was appointed to various positions throughout his life in the church, which included Minister of Music, Sunday School teacher, Bible Study teacher and Interim Pastor. He attended Harvest Light Family Ministries under the leadership of Pastor Thelma Parks where he received his license as a minister and was later ordained in 2018 as an Elder in the church. Following years of preparation, God released him to embark upon his own ministry.

He has an anointing that allows him to minister to those in need. He devotes himself to being available to members, conducting bible study, ministering to the community, organizing mission ministries and studying the word of God. He is supported in ministry by his wife, Lucinda, their four children and one grandchild. His ultimate desire is to help people find God, grow their faith, discover their purpose and then make a difference.

Website: www.LoveAllianceCF.org
Email: LoveAllianceCF@gmail.com

Additional Notes

____

____

____

____

Day 17

"God is within her, she will not fall."

Psalms 46:5 (NIV)

Day 17

Guaranteed Stability

"God is within her, she will not fall." ***Psalms 46:5 (NIV)***

When I was in High School people would often ask why I wore high heels (mostly stilettos) every day. Some would even try to make me stumble and fall. I never did because, in my mind, I was stable. I walked with the assurance that I could balance my thin frame on the tiny sticks that were glued to the bottom of the shoe.

Now that I am older and realize that wearing heels probably wasn't good for my back, I reflect on the *Psalm* that guarantees stability. I now walk with the assurance that I can balance everything on the Word of God.

Psalms 46:5 notifies the reader that God's presence provides stability. Although some versions of the scripture refer to a female, we can all walk with assurance knowing that God is able and willing to keep us from falling. This applies to everything in our lives (work, school, relationships, etc.). God guarantees us stability, but we must completely trust in Him.

Today's J.O.Y. Plan

JESUS – Study *Psalm 46* and research the background behind why this note of praise was written.

OTHERS – Share an experience of when God kept you from falling with one person today.

YOU – Take ten minutes to reflect on how God brought you through a tough situation and write down how you felt when you realized it was God who kept you stable.

Date Completed ______________________

Reflect on the Day's J.O.Y. Action Plan

Write any accomplishments, notes from study, responses from others, etc.

____

____

____

____

____

____

____

____

____

____

____

____

____

Day 17

About The Author

Courtney Crawford is the daughter of Nicole (Craig) Carter & Robert Crawford. She is a chef and an educator by training. Her identity is a growing woman of God living where God has her now but realizes that each phase is temporary. She was raised in the Baptist church singing in the choir, serving as an usher and Sunday School secretary.

She is a NC state champion long jumper who received a full athletic scholarship for Track and Field. Her scholarship paid for two degrees.

Currently Courtney studies how to be independently wealthy, while obtaining experience in every aspect of the food industry.

Additional Notes

____

____

____

____

____

____

____

____

____

____

____

____

____

Day 18

"The archers have bitterly grieved him, shot at him and hated him. But his bow remained in strength, And the arms of his hands were made strong by the hands of the Mighty God of Jacob (From there is the Shepherd, the Stone of Israel), By the God of your father who will help you, and by the Almighty who will bless you With blessings of heaven above, Blessings of the deep that lies beneath, Blessings of the breasts and of the womb." **Genesis 49:23-25 (NKJV)**

Day 18

Teamwork Makes the Dream WORK!

"The archers have bitterly grieved him, shot at him and hated him. But his bow remained in strength, And the arms of his hands were made strong by the hands of the Mighty God of Jacob (From there is the Shepherd, the Stone of Israel), By the God of your father who will help you, and by the Almighty who will bless you With blessings of heaven above, Blessings of the deep that lies beneath, Blessings of the breasts and of the womb." **Genesis 49:23-25 (NKJV)**

In *Genesis 49*, Joseph found himself celebrating the times God rescued him from the attacks of the enemy. We often struggle in life when situations arise because we feel as though we are alone. This place of loneliness is typically hard for us to overcome. The problem is that we tend to rely on our own strength in these spiritual battles. We forget that spiritual battles are there for a reason and that we have a partner that is available to help us. The help that God gave to Joseph is only a prayer away for us. We are to rely on the teamwork that the Holy Spirit gives us like God gave to Joseph. This reliance is required to overcome these battles. Teamwork makes the dream work.

The other part of the team is when we closely align ourselves with God through our faith. In the text, Joseph was able to overcome several battles, whether it was with people or in the spirit. He was able to draw closer to God as adversity mounted. In other words, when his enemies came against him, when it seemed like there was no hope for a future, he understood one thing; He could trust God to rescue him. He knew that trusting God showed great faith. Spiritual battles require teamwork. You can't do it alone. You must allow God to work through you in order to accomplish any goal successfully. Spiritual teamwork makes the *Spiritual Dream Work.*

Today's J.O.Y. Plan

JESUS – Study *Genesis 49.*

OTHERS – E-mail or Text three people encouraging them not to rely on their own strength when dealing with spiritual battles. Provide an illustration of what a spiritual battle is and ways they can fight in the spirit.

YOU – Take a walk and ask God to show you who your physical dream team (divine connections) should be in this season.

Date Completed ____________________________

Reflect on the Day's J.O.Y. Action Plan

Write any accomplishments, notes from study, responses from others, etc.

____

____

____

____

____

____

____

____

____

____

____

____

____

Day 18

About The Author

Pastor Craig Carter Sr. is the gentle giant who has a passion for shepherding God's people. His personal testimony, from "Pit to Prison to Palace" provides him the unique opportunity to reach people from all backgrounds.

He is the dedicated Pastor of Shattered Chains Christian Ministry where the mission is to provide people from all backgrounds with the tools to shatter the chains that keep us bound. Once the chains are shattered, we can be better used by God.

Craig has over 10-years of experience spiritually preaching, teaching, and counseling (eight years as an Associate Minister & two years as a Pastor). He attended Liberty University and obtained his Bachelor of Science in Religious Studies from Living Episcopal Bible College. His ordination is through the Rowan Baptist Association.

As a truck driver, Craig has the great opportunity to live his childhood dream of driving "big rigs". He is married to the former Nicole Crews, and they have nine kids and eleven grandkids. His hobbies are spending time with family, cooking/baking, gardening, and watching sports.

Facebook: www.facebook.com/ShatteredChainsChristianMinistry
Email: ChainsrShattered@gmail.com

Additional Notes

____

____

____

____

____

Day 19

"Jesus Wept."

John 11:35 (MSG)

Compassion

"Jesus Wept." ***John 11:35 (MSG)***

In the 2004 movie Barbershop 2, Calvin (played by actor Ice Cube) was about to eat a meal in front of an elderly neighbor, Miss Emma. She gets on him for not praying over his food before eating. So, Calvin jokingly says "Jesus Wept". Miss Emma then asked, Why did Jesus Weep? It wasn't until the end of the movie that Calvin responds to her question in front of a crowd at a Town Hall meeting. He gives an accurate account of what occurred with Mary, Martha, and Lazarus and stated when Jesus saw the pain that Mary and Martha felt in the death of their brother Lazarus, Jesus cried too. It was the compassion he felt. Calvin continued addressing the crowd, as a leader in his community, to stand up for those who couldn't stand up for themselves by saying that the people (referring to the current residents) didn't fit the new plan. In fact, he mentioned "The People" several times in his speech. "Once you lose the people, you lose the neighborhood."

God, in Jesus' form, illustrates the compassion that we should have for others. *1 John 4:20* tells us that we can't say we love God who we can't see and not love our brother who we can see. In other words, it is a mandate that we share in the sufferings of our brothers and sisters. We do this by having compassion. Compassion is to recognize the suffering of others and then take action to help. Compassion represents a physical expression of love for those who are suffering.

Remember, it is not a bad thing to cry, especially when we are mourning with our brothers and sisters. Jesus was weeping to show he cared. He showed compassion.

Today's J.O.Y. Plan

JESUS – Study *John 11:35, Luke 14:41-42, 1 john 4:20, Psalm 30:5* and the cross references for each.

OTHERS – Identify the last two people that you know have had issues and do something that illustrates compassion (handwritten note, lunch, coffee, etc.).

YOU – Take a moment and lament about things that aren't sitting right with you.

Date Completed ______________________________

Reflect on the Day's J.O.Y. Action Plan

Write any accomplishments, notes from study, responses from others, etc.

____

____

____

____

____

____

____

____

____

____

____

____

____

Day 19

About The Author

Nicole Crews Carter, The Ultimate J.O.Y. Leader, is known as the thermostat that changes the climate of any room. Her contagious smile illustrates the vision that God wants for everyone – true JOY. She is the Visionary Author for this project.

Website: www.EstablishingJOY.com
Email: Info@EstablishingJOY.com
Facebook: www.facebook.com/EstablishingJOY1
Instagram: www.Instagram.com/EstablishingJOY
X (formerly Twitter): www.x.com/EstablishingJOY
YouTube: www.YouTube.com/@EstablishingJOY
LinkedIn: www.linkedin.com/in/NicoleCrewsCarter
ClubHouse: www.clubhouse.com/house/Establishing-JOY

Additional Notes

Day 20

"Anna, a prophet, was also there in the temple. She was the daughter of Phanuel, from the tribe of Asher, and she was very old. Her husband died when they had been married only seven years. Then she lived as a widow to the age of 84. She never left the temple but stayed there day and night, worshiping God with fasting and prayer. She came along just as Simeon was walking with Mary and Joseph, and she began praising God. She talked about the child to everyone who had been waiting expectantly for God to rescue Jerusalem."

Luke 2:36-38(NLT)

Day 20

Ask Anna!

"Anna, a prophet, was also there in the temple. She was the daughter of Phanuel, from the tribe of Asher, and she was very old. Her husband died when they had been married only seven years. Then she lived as a widow to the age of 84. She never left the temple but stayed there day and night, worshiping God with fasting and prayer. She came along just as Simeon was walking with Mary and Joseph, and she began praising God. She talked about the child to everyone who had been waiting expectantly for God to rescue Jerusalem." **Luke 2:36-38(NLT)**

This devotion is designed to cause you to pause. After this brief but powerful devotion, you will know there are advantages and benefits to fasting, praying, and remaining with God's people. Just ask Anna.

Anna, the only named female prophet in the New Testament, was widowed around the age of 21 and remained in the temple until she was 84 years old. She helps us to think about maintaining expectancy when there seems to be no hope. Anna found hope in Jesus Christ.

Anna's people were still in bondage and needed a savior. As she prayed and fasted day after day, in the house (Temple), she believed the Savior was soon to come for her people. Could you please answer a question for me? What are you fasting, praying for, and believing will come to *your* house? Be consistent and do it for God's will and it will come to pass. Ask Anna.

Anna realized there was purpose in prayer for the salvation of her people. She teaches us today to be steadfast in prayer and fasting and to be immovable. Sharing the gospel of Jesus Christ is for the salvation of our people today. For your home, our schools, communities, cities, and the world. The Jewish people of Anna's day weren't back in Egypt, but they had essentially been sold into slavery while they dwelled in their own land. As Anna lived, worshipped, and prayed in the temple day after day, year after year, decade after decade, she had faith that a Savior would come soon.

Anna saw and recognized Jesus the Christ as a child as the Savior and knew every moment she'd spent in prayer and fasting was worth it. Salvation had finally come. Just Ask Anna.

If it seems like the answer is far away, hold on. When you know relationships need to be healed yet unforgiveness is thick enough to cut with a knife, keep praying. Don't stop fasting for your unsaved loved ones. Salvation has come. The Jewish people of Annas day weren't back in Egypt, but they had essentially been sold into slavery while they dwelled in their own land. Just Ask Anna!

Today's J.O.Y. Plan

JESUS - Read Luke 2.

OTHERS - Select 3 people and pray for them for three weeks.

YOU - Rejoice, Rejoice, Rejoice today!

Prayer: Gracious Lord, you are mighty in all your ways, and we love you for who you are! Everything you do is good and perfect. Amen

Date Completed ______________________________

Reflect on the Day's J.O.Y. Action Plan

Write any accomplishments, notes from study, responses from others, etc.

____

____

____

____

____

____

____

____

____

____

____

____

____

Day 20

About The Author

Minister Neva Brooks has combined her commitment to the calling from Christ, with her experience and expertise in mental wellness. She serves as founder and lead facilitator of "Comfort Companions," a program that teaches and establishes Mental Wellness Ministries in the Church. Her assignment is to glorify God and edify his Kingdom!

She is licensed and ordained as a minister in the Christian Faith and attends Anderson Zion Baptist Church in Anderson, Indiana. The Pastor is Cecil Golder III. God has allowed her to speak and witness on Global platforms.

As a Certified Life Coach and Registered Nurse, she spends time using her life experiences and professional career to help women who feel stuck. We navigate from the conflicts of life to places of confidence, freedom, and clarity. She does this best with nurses, in her words "I'm a nurse, I get it.!" Neva is the CEO of Diamond Sharp Coaching, LLC. and founder of Diamonds Sharpens Diamonds, a women's ministry based on the biblical principles in *Proverbs 27:17*.

Neva received nursing degrees from Anderson University and IUPUI Indianapolis. She earned a Master of Business Administration from Indiana Wesleyan University. She holds Certifications in various areas of Psychology, Mental Wellness and Behavioral Health.

She is Mother, Nana, Sister, Daughter, and true Sister-Friend, who loves her family.

Website: www.DiamondSharpCoach.com
Email: DiamonSharpCoach@gmail.com

Additional Notes

____

____

____

Day 21

"A body isn't just a single part blown up into something huge. It's all the different-but-similar parts arranged and functioning together......If Ear said, "I'm not beautiful like Eye, transparent and expressive; I don't deserve a place on the head," would you want to remove it from the body? If the body was all eye, how could it hear? If all ear, how could it smell? As it is, we see that God has carefully placed each part of the body right where he wanted it."

1 Corinthians 12:14-18 (MSG)

I'm Different – By Design!

"A body isn't just a single part blown up into something huge. It's all the different-but-similar parts arranged and functioning together. If Foot said, "I'm not elegant like Hand, embellished with rings; I guess I don't belong to this body," would that make it so? If Ear said, "I'm not beautiful like Eye, transparent and expressive; I don't deserve a place on the head," would you want to remove it from the body? If the body was all eye, how could it hear? If all ear, how could it smell? As it is, we see that God has carefully placed each part of the body right where he wanted it." ***1 Corinthians 12:14-18 (MSG)***

What happens when you try to put a square peg in a round hole? Better yet, have you ever attempted to complete a 1000-piece puzzle? And in your frustration, you try to force a piece into a space it doesn't belong to. If you can force it in place, you still can't complete the puzzle because a piece is out of place. That piece can only fit in the space that was customed *By Design*.

The same is true with every body part of the human body. The heart cannot do the job that the liver is designed to do. Additionally, we would look crazy if we walked around on our hands all day. Although both the eye and the ear begin with e and only have three letters, their functions are completely different. God uniquely designed each human body part and each human being differently for a specific purpose *By Design*.

Romans 12:2 tells us to not be conformed to this world. We should challenge ourselves to view things the way that God does and allow the Holy Spirit to transform our minds so we can recognize His will for our individual lives. The way that someone else has done things in the past typically isn't what God is calling you to do now. Grab hold of the fact that you are different because it is *By God's Design*.

Today's J.O.Y. Plan

JESUS – Study the meaning behind the example given in *1 Corinthians 12* and ask God to reveal what it means to you in this season of your life.

OTHERS – Identify two people that you have struggled to understand in the past and have a conversation about their differences and why it's important for each of us to know God's will for our lives.

YOU – Identify the one thing that you don't like about yourself (or one thing you wish was different) and begin to praise God for how He is using that thing to keep you closer to Him. *"All things work together for the good." Romans 8:28*

Date Completed ____________________________

Reflect on the Day's J.O.Y. Action Plan

Write any accomplishments, notes from study, responses from others, etc.

____

____

____

____

____

____

____

____

____

____

____

Day 21

About The Author

Nicole Crews Carter, The Ultimate J.O.Y. Leader, is known as the thermostat that changes the climate of any room. Her contagious smile illustrates the vision that God wants for everyone – true JOY. She is the Visionary Author for this project.

Website: www.EstablishingJOY.com
Email: Info@EstablishingJOY.com
Facebook: www.facebook.com/EstablishingJOY1
Instagram: www.Instagram.com/EstablishingJOY
X (formerly Twitter): www.x.com/EstablishingJOY
YouTube: www.YouTube.com/@EstablishingJOY
LinkedIn: www.linkedin.com/in/NicoleCrewsCarter
ClubHouse: www.clubhouse.com/house/Establishing-JOY

Additional Notes

___

___

___

___

___

___

___

___

___

___

___

___

Continue Your Personal JOurneY

There are multiple ways to ensure that the J.O.Y. in your personal JOurneY continues. Check out the latest opportunities by going to the website www.EstablishingJOY.com or by joining our mailing list at info@EstablishingJOY.com.

Also if you desire to join the next 21-day Devotional please contact us via e-mail.

Other books by Nicole Crews Carter

- Establishing J.O.Y.
- J.O.Y. as a Single Mom
- Morning J.O.Y. Planner
- Morning J.O.Y. 21 – day Devotional Volume One

Made in the USA
Columbia, SC
29 September 2023

23576646R00054